EVERYTHING IS IMPORTANT UNTIL NOTHING IS IMPORTANT

EVERYTHING IS IMPORTANT UNTIL NOTHING IS IMPORTANT

Poems by
John Ellison

© 2015–2022 by John Ellison

All rights reserved. Printed in the United States of America. No part of this book may be used or reproduced in any manner whatsoever without written permission except in the case of brief quotations embodied in critical articles or reviews. For more information, contact johne.goatpalacezine@gmail.com.

Goat Palace and Goat Palace Zine are imprints of Speak4Peace.

Front cover photo ("Untitled") © Annie Spratt/Unsplash.com (@anniespratt and anniespratt.com). Back cover art from Canva.com. Used by permission. All rights reserved.

Kim Stafford quotation from *The Muse Is Among Us: Eloquent Listening and Other Pleasures of the Writer's Craft*, University of Georgia Press, 2003.

ISBN 978-0-9828662-2-1

Library of Congress Control Number: 2021905359

Book and cover design by L. Link.

Goat Palace logo by R. Turner.

Please see page 143 for more information about Goat Palace Zine.

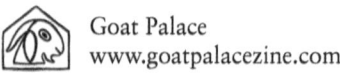
Goat Palace
www.goatpalacezine.com

For my beloved Lesley
through whom my real life began
so long ago, now into forever

EVERYTHING IS IMPORTANT
UNTIL NOTHING IS IMPORTANT

CONTENTS

A few introductory thoughts *xiii*
How the river got its name *xviii*

The Poems
In January 3
Make even the frost holy 4
The way is long and hard 5
Empty days 6
A fire is about shapes 7
Song 8
Remember 9
Whether we live or die 11
Us 13
Gone 15
Until you died 16
Unfinished fragment 17
Tell me the story again 18
Echo 20
The dream 21
Counting airplanes 22
Open the book 23
From my notebook I 25
Artifact 26
At the last 27
Wounds 29
Breathe I 31
Bells 32
Breathe II 33
Grief 34

Just Guessing 36
Unnamed 38
Prayer 39
Sing 40
Something so small 41
Confession 43
When I think about love 45
You always say yes 47
Down on the cancer floor 49
Your name 50
Scar tissue 53
Suddenly 54
Open thy hand 55
Before I say a word 56
Memory 57
Untitled fragment I 60
Drift away (a lullaby) 61
Like light 63
Another song 64
The eyes of others 65
Shining thing 66
Black star 67
The fixation 68
The silver forest 69
Blue 70
Rice 71
Midstream 72
From my notebook II 73
Coming for you 74
Faded light 75
Let it be gone 76
Out in the stars 77
Untitled fragments 78

You never ask, I never speak 79
Thoughts at night 81
Checking for angels 82
All for your name 84
Places in my heart 85
Prayer wheel 86
Untitled fragment II 88
The fall 89
Winter 91
Lost and found 92
Memories on a map 93
Safe 94
The beauty of rain 95
Return to blue 96
Cold wave 97
Tonight 98
One time tender 99
Standing in the dark 100
How words fit together 101
The memory 102
Sweet talk 103
Angel 104
Turning home 105
From darkness to darkness 106
Late walk in winter 107
Purity 108
Death in the age of texting 109
Empty 110
Untitled fragment III 111
All the bad words 112
Almost falling 113
Lines soften 114
A fire in dry grass 115

Soft as skin *116*
The pool *117*
A place to start *118*
Ohio *119*
Singing still *121*
Beside the blue lake *122*
Like fire *123*
"Shooting Jesus" *124*
Wanderer *125*
What we tell ourselves *126*
Sand angel *127*
The promise *128*
Glass *129*
Ashes *130*
Into the hardest night *131*
Sleep will come *132*
These memories *133*
Night *134*
Broken stones *135*
To die *137*
The cooling heart *138*
Breath of the stars *139*
At the end of my time *140*

The whole world is a scene: About Goat Palace *143*

A few introductory thoughts

Song lyrics and poetry are half-siblings. It's like they share one parent, and no one in the family is totally happy about that. The "family," meaning everyone who loves poetry *and* songs, has spent hundreds of years arguing about which one is the "legitimate" child, and which one is the "outcast." The more elaborate the argument, for either case, the more suspicion grows.

That's how I've viewed song lyrics practically my whole life. Not *real* poetry. But I love both. Even with the *best* masters of songwriting, including Nobel Laureate Bob Dylan's magisterial output, for example, when he was recognized in 2016 as a Nobel *poet*, I held back calling his work *real* poetry, for a time. Not anymore. (If you think it's easy doing what Dylan does as a writer, try writing *one* song in the "style" of Dylan. It's much harder than you'd think.) Loving both was a problem. So it was time to rethink the question of legitimacy.

Everything changed for me in 2012 when a friend sent me a playlist with the song "California Zephyr," written by Jay Farrar (Son Volt) and Benjamin Gibbard (Death Cab for Cutie). "California Zephyr" is a "song," but with "lyrics" drawn from the 1962 novel *Big Sur* by Jack Kerouac. The *music* is Farrar and Gibbard; the *lyrics* are all Kerouac. And that *one* song, along with the 11 others that make up a record (and the documentary film that goes with it) called "One Fast Move or I'm Gone: Music from Kerouac's *Big Sur*" (Atlantic, 2009), changed my thinking about what makes a poem and what makes a song.

It was a transformative listening experience. I played that record over and over. Not even the word "transformative" is big enough to express how I felt at the time, hearing all those amazing songs the first time. I couldn't believe such a thing could be done. It was as if Kerouac's words had grown wings.

Other people have done this kind of thing before Farrar and Gibbard did it using *Big Sur,* using prose or poetry other than Kerouac's, of course, to find lyrics for other songs. But this was a first for me. This record burned down to the ground all my fancy arguments about why lyrics and poems are two separate things, instead of being *one* thing, one family.

I put "One Fast Move or I'm Gone" on just now as I'm writing this. It's a *perfect* record. I wonder if others were knocked out by it like I was. I hope so. Hearing it again now takes me back to that lightning strike day when every "Kerouac" song made me see and hear lyrics *and* poetry in a whole new way.

I became possessed. I started writing poems as songs, almost immediately and ended up with more than 200 songs (just the lyrics). It was freeing. I've written poetry all my life. I just never showed it to anyone or kept much of it. I've burned more than a couple notebooks of my writing over the years.

After writing my "songs" for almost a year, I tried to get some of my work made into real "songs," working with local musicians and a friend who was sort of "co-producing" the project with me. Although the record never got made, I kept writing. Then, I noticed something changing as I wrote. My "songs" were slowly becoming something sharper, shorter, more like how I've always thought poetry should be. Slowly, I let my "songs" turn back into "poems," and my desire to make a record faded.

As I look over this collection, I can no longer see where the earliest poems walked away from the need for musicians to make them real. It just happened. They started standing by themselves. They wanted to be seen as poems. The poems that appear early in this collection still have that "song" feeling for me. The later ones feel more like they're happy being poems as they are. Of course, I now know music could be added to *any* of them (almost) and they could be songs, too. The change is inside *me* now, not inside them.

    Most of these poems found their way to friends in proper letters, still my favorite way of communicating, starting in late 2015 into early 2016, the year I was diagnosed with cancer. You'll see the darkness creeping into my images and the anger rising. Cancer changes everything. (Surviving it means you get more time to think about it and worry.) It divided my life into two halves: "BC" (before cancer), and "AC" (after cancer). BC, I worked very hard trying to get my "lyrics" into songs with working musicians to make records. Then cancer arrived and took over everything for more than two years. (I'm a "cancer survivor" now, so that's good.) I felt sad not making records, but cancer helped me see into my disappointment and helped me to accept more and to keep writing.

    I found myself letting go of lots of things, ideas about my present and future self. It's not so much about lowering standards. It's more about accepting that time is short. It's hard to keep worrying about all the things you can't control, especially the things you'll never finish. My lists got shorter and more doable.

    There's definitely a cancer vibe in this book, almost a journal as I read these poems now, gathered in one place for the first time. Some of these pieces I had forgotten.

    Perhaps I should say a few final words about my writing process, such as it is, after rejecting the whole notion of separate worlds of writing poems and writing songs. In the beginning, when I was striving to write what I thought of as "song lyrics," it was a direct process of working out ideas. I saw a destination, a record, that I was hoping to create. Even then, I've never felt that I summon my writing. Rather, it summons me.

Music was always there as source and inspiration, as much as a destination. I absorbed records as I searched them out as a songwriter. Even though I'd abandoned vinyl records years before this work, I immediately returned to vinyl as I rushed to create a body of work from which I could draw out *my* record. I built an enormous collection of LPs, CDs, and cassettes. Together with my wife, Lesley, we started a vinyl record label (Untide Records).

For this reason, you'll see something added here. As I wrote song lyrics, I built playlists for inspiration. Then, as the songs turned back into poems, I started creating *playlists* associated with specific poems. It was a spontaneous thing.

When it fit, as I assembled this poetry collection, I included these playlists, "touch points," as a kind of window into some of my poems, when they connected. These playlists were built *after* I'd written each poem. I didn't use anything from these songs as I was writing. It was sort of a reverse process of what Farrar and Gibbard had done.

However, when I started doing this, I realized something new was happening. By working backward, using the poem as the starting point, toward a collection of songs that I connected with, I found myself understanding better what I'd written.

Maybe it's the same thing that happens to some musicians when they release records. Sometimes you hear that recording artists say they *learn* how their songs want to be played as they tour and play them live.

Today, I think of myself as a poet, not a songwriter, simply because I have to loosely work with the labels we give ourselves. It's a shorthand, nothing more. But now when I read the luminous work of poets like Frank Stanford (1948–1978) and Edward Thomas 1878–1917), two lodestar spirits I use to navigate "the old ways" of poetry, I find them easy company, along with my records, all outsiders doing what we do, using but resisting labels of what these things mean as we create them.

Poems and song lyrics walk side by side for me now. Each possesses unique properties that enrich our lives. We can use them together to explore the emotional pathways we all must cross in our lives. Neither is grander than the other. If I taught a poetry class, I'd begin each class by playing a few records to open each discussion. As Bruce Springsteen once wrote, you can learn more about life in a three-minute song than you can from years in school.

Songs and poems have become reunited. That's how I see this book, and that's how I live now with these two timeless forms of storytelling.

How the river got its name

"Life is a river of stories."
—Kim Stafford

There's a river
　near here
　　called "The Perfect Moment."

It was called that by people
　who are gone now,
　　but they're still with us.

Rivers and people
　traveling, naming things as we go.
　　This river is ours.
We float along with each other.

Some people say
　names are just names, places are just places.
　　But that's like saying memories are just
　　　memories.
Or love is just love.

We started all this naming with the Moment.
　The Perfect Moment *is* The Perfect Moment.
　　Nothing stays the same.
But there's enough.

And, just think…
　What we can do with all we still have.

THE POEMS

In January

Being water, being rain
and finally getting to be snow
making her body lace
I forget how the line goes
something about singing
while the years turn into birds
I sure wish I could remember
how it went because you loved
to make snow angels
every time it snowed
in January

Playlist
"Cynthia's in Love" (Carroll Gibbons & The Savoy Hotel Orpheans), "The Sun Is Shining Down" (JJ Grey & Mofro), "Underwear" (Pulp), "Misty Blue" (Dorothy Moore), "The Parting Glass" (Emily Kinney & Lauren Cohan), "Common Man" (David Ruffin), "Encounter at 3 AM" (Clem Snide), "Crying Out Loud (Tears of Joy)" (The Soledad Brothers), "Reason to Believe" (Tim Hardin), "Trapped by a Thing Called Love" (Denise LaSalle), "We Ride" (Missy Higgins), "Tomorrow I Will Be Yours" (Paula Cole Band), "Wichita Lineman" (Linda Bruner), "Bright Light" (Mount Moriah), "I Can't Forget" (Jarvis Cocker), "Move It" (Cliff Richard), "Bird on a String" (Evergreen), "I Wish It Would Rain" (Mayer Hawthorne), "Stay with Me Baby" (Duffy), "One More Lonely Night" (Maurice Hayes), "Start Anew" (Beady Eye)

Make even the frost holy

The everyday winter
sun comes cold
like a wave like another wave
small, still, returning home
and with each
I'm filled with
love
for the lonely wind
and the wandering hour
and songs written long ago
for this arc of thin light
for the wave, for the wood dove
holding each other
love
the burning center
of all things

The way is long and hard

Like who?
neither remembers
but hammers
stubborn gold
from mesa skies,
like years do
because heat
makes the rules
for maps
and for memories,
like poor who?
you moon
hating being
another mirror
forever and never
again to be
new

Empty days

My words are ordinary
like rain
as I work my hard edges
of what it means to pretend to love
these empty days
left over
long after the miles of rusted road
have been crossed
I wonder
what does it feel like
to be sure?

A fire is about shapes

A fire is about shapes
locking mechanisms
and cradles

a fire is about movement
red cities
and ruins

a fire is about peace
end of memories
and forgetting

a fire is about failure
standing still
and waiting

a fire is about despair
turning away
and going down

a fire is about night
shadow keys
and no way out

a fire is about names
walls, stone, trees
and warm, warm rain

Song

Like a ruin
of cities or tools
your hands
make the skin
of the sea of
time itself
stop moving
allowing my breath
to pause and
say yes before
the song singing
stops playing
and dies

Remember

Remember, we were younger
smoking cheaper cigarettes
walking under colder stars

talking about drummers
talking about dead singers
talking about bands
and songs about cars
we thought we should like

I think I said
I was wrong then, I was wrong
about almost everything
I thought back then

about my back-to-back years
sleeping in houses I burned down
to the ground, forever looking
backward and still
my time is running out

you said we all come from
a place, and you said
we all have to live someplace

so, we desperately
fall in love with anyone
in airports, with faces we hope
can make our flights feel safer

you said
everyone feels the same
about everyone they meet
in airports

about love and loss
about living day to day, in darkness
exhausted by the way the things
we build always crash down
and bury us

so, I need to say it out loud
I was wrong, I was wrong, I was wrong
because everything breaks
as everything changes
and everyone has to leave home

and you said stop counting
just say your name out loud
from time to time

you said counting things like
cigarettes or miles,
lovers, or dead-end jobs
is just asking for trouble
asking for more trouble
to come

Whether we live or die

We'll hold hands in the rain
the trains will all run on time
we'll walk around Trafalgar Square
we'll feed the lions, pray for the lambs

whether we live or die
we'll read the paper in the rain
all the clocks will run on time
we'll feed the pigeons, pray for the homeless

whether we live or die
we'll go cycling in the rain
all the wheels will turn on time
we'll read our maps, pray for angels

whether we live or die
we'll be home in the rain
all the runners will finish on time
we'll write our books, pray for peace

we'll wear our political pins, pray for night
we'll hold our breath, pray for sleep
we'll stop our hearts, pray for release
whether we live or die

Playlist
"How High the Moon" (Dianne Reeves), "Masters of War"
(Lucinda Williams/Charles Lloyd & The Marvels), "Ohio"
(Over the Rhine), "Ask Her for Water" (T-Model Ford),
"St. Louis Gal" (Cécile McLorin Salvant), "Sao Paulo"

(Deadstring Brothers), "Death Letter" (Cassandra Wilson), "On My Way" (Luke Winslow-King), "Sugar" (Editors), "Same to You" (Lydia Loveless), "It's Morning Irene" (Deadstring Brothers), "Sad Days Lonely Nights" (Spiritualized), "Love Letters" (Dex Romweber Duo), "Wine Lips" (Lydia Loveless), "Gonna Miss You When You're Gone" (Patty Griffin), "Tears of Joy" (Etta James), "Champagne Carolla" (Justin Towns Earle), "North of Alabama by Mornin'" (Bobby Bare, Jr.), "Hickory Wind" (Lucinda Williams/Buddy Miller & Friends)

Us

Everything is
important until
nothing's important
except us
everything is
the same until
everything changes
except us

*

There's a fire someplace
off in the trees
smoke on a weathering breeze
silence on a grieving
sea

islands speak
something in their names
something about what it means
to stay even when there's nothing new to say
about the sea

you burned a heart
into the wood of your guitar
with a melodic thorn to pierce
your heart to feel
but only when you play

I remember your song
but not the fragrant love
it was never my forest song

and it was all a long, long
time ago

*

Everything
is important
until nothing
is important
except us

everything
is the same
until everything
changes
except us

Playlist
"The Crane Wife 3" (Marianne Faithfull), "Hurt a Little
While" (Patty Griffin), "Goodbye" (The Pretenders),
"Suspicious Minds" (My Morning Jacket), "Slick & Delta
Queen" (Kyle Craft), "She Ain't a Child No More" (Sharon
Jones & The Dap Kings), "Miracle Temple Holiness"
(Mount Moriah), "King Hummingbird" (JJ Grey & Mofro),
"Snake Charmer" (Patty Griffin), "Joy" (Loma), "His
Master's Voice" (Monsters of Folk), "Shake Yo' Bottle"
(Etta James), "Ohio" (Patty Griffin), "(I'm) Like a Rolling
Stone" (Titus Andronicus), "Gold Calf Moan" (Kyle Craft),
"Your Thins Is a Drag" (Sharon Jones & The Dap Kings),
"Crash into the Sun" (Jim White), "Funny How Time Slips
Away" (Jim James), "Love That Burns" (Fleetwood Mac),
"Killin' It" (R. Turner), "Won't Be the Last Time" (Justin
Townes Earle), "Arabella" (Ha Ha Tonka), "On My Way"
(Luke Winslow-King)

Gone

Sinking into
the silence of names
and the unbearable
shadows of love
love once alive inside
flame overwhelms me
and pulls me
back hard then
leaves me
in rain-shimmering
heat on a familiar
dry road without
a returning, hardly
believing there can be
an end
of singing
an end
of the story
of your names
of your love
your hands
your song
gone

Until you died

They open and they close
the shadows I know
then I lose
the years same as photographs
they meant something
to you, to me, a shared something
for reasons more
than we were asking back then
the war you never talked about
that I never stopped talking about
you said *no*
then you turned on
the radio and mowed the lawn

in my memory every summer
I hear your radio, a ballgame
play by play, on the picnic table
until you died
of cancer in a building
I still drive by, when I have the time

Unfinished fragment

The good and the bad together
is the definition of life
in a mirror

I want to love all of it
but it's hard to live
in a mirror

it seems so natural to fight
against the moment
moment after moment after moment

water
is the most powerful thing on earth
because it has no memory

Tell me the story again

When the land caught fire
and our lives burned down cold
when the rain cut the glass
and the nights turned us away alone
you were the sea
tell me the story again

*

when our eyes lost the stars
when our hands wouldn't hold
when our hearts made us old
when our words left us alone
you were the lightning
tell me the story again

*

when the streets stopped time
when frost froze the voices of the trees
when nothing could save us
when no one could remember for us
you were the stone in the stream
tell me the story again

Playlist
"Power of My Love" (Jack White), "L.A. County Jail Blues" (Cypress Grove), "City in Pain" (Nick Cave), "This Is Yesterday" (Manic Street Preachers), "Lemonade Stand Blues" (Ricky Turner), "I'm New Here" (Gil Scott-Heron), "Hypnotized" (Dream Police), "Sleeping Man" (Vic Chesnutt), "Chelsea Hotel #2" (Kyle Craft), "A Spanish Incident"

(Michael Chapman), "When I Get Back" (Handsome Furs), "Howlin'" (Slug Guts), "I Need Something New" (Savages), "Living in Doubt" (Marching Church), "Squeeki Tiki" (The Coathangers), "Heads or Tails" (Eagulls), "Corina, Corina" (Ralph White), "Funny How Time Slips Away" (Jim James)

Echo

You text me, there's an echo someplace else
you still remember, but I need to forget

you ask me why, you're always someplace else
you still tremble, but everyone forgets

we were something then, very nearly perfect
we were two love songs, but it was a long time ago

*

you touch me, there's an echo someplace else
you asked me to leave, so I left

you never promised me, happiness is always
    someplace else
you asked me to believe, by then there was nothing left

we were something then, very nearly perfect
we were the best of friends, but it was a long time ago

*

you moved away from me, there's an echo someplace else
you live your life without me, I carry the weight of
    lost time

you have your stories, I have mine
you found something else, I need to forget

we were something then, very nearly perfect
we can't listen to those songs anymore

it was a long, long time ago

The dream

There's rain
this cold storm's
not forgiving

giving pain
a warm memory's voice
just by living

and still, like
forgiving, there's
singing

Counting airplanes

And suddenly
there you are
standing before me
in an old gray raincoat
and I remember
driving through the valley
counting the signs
announcing each field's crop
chop, corn, alfalfa, wheat
but we might as well have been
counting airplanes
some fields were late
some were burning
and with every counting
you unlocked me

Open the book

Start again
open the book
come home again
be you again
just open the book

open the book
breathe easy again
feel alive again
be certain again
be strong again
just open the book

time after time
this is just how it goes
love after love
this is what we pay
year after year
this is what we carry
sorrow after sorrow
this is where our faith goes
to love and be loved

that's all there is
to love and be loved
and not turn away
not turn away
to love and be loved
this is the price
we all pay

so open your book
you can start again
you can walk back again
open your book
and you can be you again
just open your book

so, open your book
you will feel it all again
you can go home again
and live again
together, we'll start again
and live again

From my notebook I

If you want to be a person with faith in what comes next, you have to understand one very difficult thing: *the cost of love*. It doesn't matter what tools you use to get there. Those are just the tools. Hate is easy. Love is hard.

Artifact

Love the dead
love all the dead
remember every face
every dying place
and the sound of every voice
their hair and their hands
and the way they return
to you
when you hear a song
you didn't know
but that sounds like it comes
from inside you someplace
like a name
like a light
like a clock
like a warning

Playlist
"Iron Sky" (Paolo Nutini), "Fear Is Like Fire (Live)" (Fink), "Fighter Pilot" (Sanders Bohlke), "Always Gold" (Radical Face), "Switzerland" (Daughter), "Grace" (Jeff Buckley), "Don't Look Back in Anger" (Oasis), "Atmosphere" (Joy Division), "Parasite" (Nicked Drake), "Run Me Out" (Zola Jesus), "Lampshades on Fire" (Modest Mouse), "Live Forever" (Drew Holcomb and The Neighbors), "Déjà Vu" (Roger Waters), "I Found You" (Alabama Shakes), "Travelin' On" (Norah Jones)

At the last

At the last
all we know
of our time
our mother
our father
or any other
mother or father
is all they know
about their time
about their creator

at the last
time softly gently
endlessly tirelessly
bleeds us away
time all our dead
language
lost forever buried
memory about how
we came
to fail love

at the last
we don't speak
we can't speak
we won't speak
still we repeat
how we fail
love

until years after
when alone we find
a slipper
under a dresser
a broken fountain
pen
or a photograph
of someplace else

at the last
we all let
the darkness
come
grateful everything emptying
letting all our shadows
fears tears bad decisions
broken years
slip away

except the softly
touching undying
tenacity
of how we all
failed love

Wounds

A life based on numbers
is like a needle pushed slowly into the skin
it's difficult to know where to begin
to explain the waterfall of pain in counting
and how it holds you aloft while also
reminding you how everything else descends
like empty shells washed up on beaches
after our final night of tides and winds
no one remembers the dark currents of pain
that pull us from shore bruising every surface
when dreams and the sea come up empty
we just get smaller while we wait breathless
for answers from the movements of machines
that never pretend they care who we are
or know the difference between love and fear
when life is something only for the counting

Playlist
"Walking with the Beast" (Primal Scream), "Every Time the Sun Comes Up" (Sharon Van Etten), "Turbine" (Barbarossa), "Love That Burns" (Fleetwood Mac), "Ain't That Lovin' You Baby" (Thin White Rope), "The Weary Kind" (Ryan Bingham), "I'm Not Afraid to Die" (Gillian Welch), "21 York Street" (And Also the Trees), "What Death Leaves Behind" (Los Campesinos!), "Guns of Umpqua" (Drive-By Truckers), "Dreaming My Dreams" (Cowboy Junkies), "Never Never Blues" (John Trudell), "Hunt Me Down" (The Black Angels), "Three Candles" (Kyle Craft), "You Are the Wilderness" (Voxhaul Broadcast), "Cemetery Gaits" (Los Campesinos!), "Let the Day Begin" (The Call), "Jet Tone Boogie" (The Flat

Duo Jets), "Blue Light, Red Light (Someone's There)" (Jack White), "Lay and Love" (Bonnie "Prince" Billy), "I Whale" (Mount Eerie), "Glass Bones" (Shearwater), "Train of Love" (Bob Dylan), "Into the Fire" (Nick Cave/Debbie Harry), "A Swim in the Ocean" (The Call), "DIG, LAZARUS, DIG!!!" (Nick Cave & The Bad Seeds), "Take Me to Tomorrow" (Dave Matthews), "That's Life, Tho (Almost Hate to Say)" (Kurt Vile), "Storms" (Matt Sweeney/ Bonnie "Prince" Billy), "Bloodlines" (Barbarossa), "Don't Let Me Down" (Linda Bruner)

Breathe I

The bridge, the light, the dark
all smell like bells

her eyes have become snow
remember, all of it was real

Bells

In the sun
bells sound
like flowers
smell *both*
the color
of your eyes

Breathe II

I breathe you
and you breathe me
and we enter each other
and we leave each other
the air making us free
but we're never free
just you just me
in winter hoping
for spring then summer then
fall like a prayer
we can't speak out loud
because if we do
if we do
we'd die

Grief

Grief
is a boat
on the shore
waiting

you get in the boat
you put your hand
into the darkening water

and all you feel is the cold
you can feel ice forming all around
like pieces of your fallen sky

high overhead
birds cut their way alone
their wings look like knives

but you still can't go
back to that place to say
goodbye

and you still can't stay
to wait for anyone to come and wave
goodbye

grief
is a boat
on the shore
waiting for you

you pull your hand
out of the darkening water
and you pull your coat close
but all you feel is the cold
and the ice is still forming all around
you like pieces of your fallen sky

*

all you feel is the cold
and the ice is forming all around
you like pieces of your fallen sky

grief
is a boat
on the shore
waiting

to take you away

Just guessing

I'm just guessing
but tonight just might be
the last night
I'll ever write about love

I'm just guessing
but it can be so depressing
imagining the sound
needing someone's listening
writing but not feeling their longing
for love

I'm just guessing
but it's there when you're singing
your night-bird song
soon for sleeping
your skin so close to glowing
for love

I'm just guessing
my words trying hard but missing
my feeling confusing
what's left of my meaning
instead they're closer to being stars
far falling
for love

I'm just guessing
every cloud and every planet sailing
they know more than they're saying
silent but I'm asking

hiding and I'm writing
laughing and I'm serious
about love

I'm just guessing
but tonight just might be
my very last night trying
the very last night that I
ever write about love

Unnamed

A name like killing love
with rain and years
but *not*
forgetting the lines
so many lines
a jagged meditation
palms up like a prayer
of doubt of loss
it all doubles back
tired and not free
that shadowy thing
we can't talk about
without love

Prayer

Snow won't stop it
cancer won't stop it
this feeling that our time
is everything
is our blood pumping
telling us the same stories
over and over until
like the smell of wood smoke
and the ambient sea these things
promise us they won't die
but will return winter after winter
to find us and bring us
home

Sing

The sound of rain
whispering like rooms
at dawn
you
this place is yours
now take it make it
sing
like a stone
dreaming of a river
like a hand
soft as a wing
like a sadness
past remembering

Something so small

I'd cut myself
open
if I thought
it might help
anyone's
escape from so many
terrible days ahead
but
in my mirror
my tormented face
burns whiter in bright
light, everything feels
weaker sadder fainter
like a shiver

so
get the fuck
out of my head
because
I need the space
for something small
to remember you
by
is all I'm saying

outside
the rain
is like some perfect sound
of saying goodbye

the sound
is like some perfect pain
like believing in
goodbyes

outside
the wind
is like some perfect sound
of impatient
wandering
it isn't like the endless waiting
saying goodbye
is like some perfect pain
like never asking
why

inside
I'm always asking
questions I can't say out loud
at 3 AM
guessing and obsessing
like you
over some way
to say to you
what I never say

Confession

I'm high tonight
I'm alive tonight
remembering
all the perfect green
all the impossible blue
and the sight of your
small cheap coffin
going slowly down
going slowly down
into forever
thinking how you made
me work so hard
to hate you

but I'm high tonight
and that's all
I remember now
such a long time ago
when love was neither
being together
or being alone
comfortable in the cold
wind and the rain
when we ran out
of time and the cold wind

sent you into
the ground and everyone
else into their cars
and all the memories
blended us together
without you

but now I'm like you
I'm high tonight
wishing this night
will never end
wishing this high
will never end
but they do
with or without
our ever having said
anything like goodbye
just you and me alone
sharing tonight apart
how it feels to
learn how to die
on your own
because it's easier
than ever admitting
I was always like you
admitting what you took
with you into the ground
is all you had to give to me
to get me through
anything like
tonight

When I think about love

I think about your tiger's eyes
I think about your hands floating
like clouds in a painting
holding their starry night spinning

when I think about love
I think about a forest of ideas burning
I think about how when we're together
    we become candles
I think about driving to the river to that place
where it floods every year
and nothing bad ever happens

when I think about love
I think about the taste of your mouth
after all your strawberries have been eaten
I think about the night you gave me your wings
I think about the time when the meadow grass was
    driven by the wind
bending over a mirror of water
like every blade of grass was breathing
as the same air made our skin glisten

when I think about love
I think about being satellites flying
high over everyone's heads while they're sleeping
I think about you softly breathing and dreaming
I think about the songs you're always singing

when I think about love
I think about all the little things about you I can name
and all the big things you're never afraid of

and all the perfect moments hidden I believe in
and all the scary things we've beaten
and will go on beating
and going on and on and on

You always say yes

You always say yes
when you
should say no

I write everything down
easy as words
and still you hide in
light

I bore everyone with
the same stories
night after night

everyone's slowing down
I should know when
something is done

you always say yes
when you
should say no

I promised I'd call
before I got in my car
I promised I'd say
something better

I always write things down
when I should just forget them
there's a place for me
but it's not here

you always say yes
when you
should say no

Down on the cancer floor

I'm still waiting and it's still waiting and they're
 still waiting
in the basement where no one goes
with their fancy carpets and their softer chairs
 and their helpful pamphlets
down on the cancer floor
down on the cancer floor

and my machine's waiting and my drug's waiting
 and my needle's waiting
but the songs are all wrong
with their unbearable kindness and all their free
 bad coffee
down on the cancer floor
down on the cancer floor

but time's not waiting and fear's not waiting and
 hope's not waiting
just professional pain in the therapeutic shadows
and still, still, they need me to believe
down on the cancer floor
down on the cancer floor

Your name

Sometimes
just saying your name
is impossible for me to get out
impossible for me
to form the sound in my mouth
impossible for my heart
to allow
to hear your name aloud
coming out of my body
out of my blood
out of my memory
out of my soul
into the cold winter air
where it would freeze
and fall to the ground
a broken thing
in a cold hard place
where it would shatter
making a completely different sound
as it broke apart
into a thousand tiny pieces
of ice
to slowly melt
into the cold wet earth at my feet
while I watch

while I hold my breath
another kind of death
waiting for all the tiny pieces
of ice

to finally disappear
which would take forever
and ever
while I wait

sometimes
I think about all the times
I said your name
not giving it a thought
like breathing
like laughing
like cutting a yellow rose
your favorite rose
in our garden in June
remembering how
back then
the sound of your name
flew into the sky
and joyfully circled over my head
like a bird
and I remember watching
as the clouds
flew down low
just to be near the sound
of your name
like they do when the birds
fly up high for joy

because they can
because the clouds
need to feel the wings
of the birds
touch their bodies

now
the memory
of the sound of your name
is all I have
and I remember
and remain silent

Scar tissue

A vertical sense of loss
begins with a dying acceptance
of illusion
inside, walking the streets
seeing the cold wet streets
as they are
mirrors rather than scripture
learning to let it all go
dying becomes healing

Suddenly

We enter love
candle by candle
with the flickering memory of
fear like a child's in the dark
stones under every step

go ahead laugh
but we're always free
to hate the night
or all the air between us

or just fall in love
with every imperfect hour
with the vanishing of all time
and our fading hold

until we dream and sing
suddenly like memory unbidden
in our singular light

Open thy hand

Drift the time
be cold the air
dreams in water
is to ache, to ache
because breathing
isn't living
wait
and see

Before I say a word

My dreams have all turned
    to soft kisses on my forehead
being alive is my passion now
    and listening to the rain
through an open car window
    let's stop, get out, and walk
wander to tai tung's in the rain
    one more time, cold as it is
and talk about our lost city
    we know it's gone but we still love
it all the same, because
    in my memory, in yours, you
always know what I mean
    before I say a word

Memory

Come spring, I said
I'd remember
all that she said,
it's here, on this paper

come summer, I said
we had to be over
all that we did to get closer,
it's here, on this stone

now, we're talking about fall
our nights are coming faster
somehow, we got behind our walls
it's all coming faster

because the time
means nothing,
nothing, and
memory is everything

because the cost
means nothing
nothing, and
memory is forever

*

when the rains come
I hope I'll know what I should do
she always said I'd know
what I should do

when the frost comes
I hope I'll know what I should take
she always said I'd know
what I should take

because the time
means nothing,
nothing, and
memory is everything

because the sadness
means nothing,
nothing, and
love is forever

so I wrote everything down
she said I'd be sorry
if I didn't
write it all down

come spring, I said
I'd remember
everything she said,
it's here on my paper

come winter, I said
I would be ready
everything that's gone,
it's here on my stone

because the time
means nothing,

nothing, and
memory is everything

because the sadness
means nothing,
nothing, and
love is forever

Untitled fragment I

It's a long journey
from broken to fixed
answering questions
you can't ask
because every answer's
the same: *maybe*

Drift away (a lullaby)

I know you're tired tonight
I know you've come a long way
tonight

it's in your eyes
the mystery, the weight
the road, I can feel your sadness
the questions in your eyes

tonight, you can
drift away

your longing
rest it here tonight
with the stars, reaching down
tonight

put it all down, close your eyes
you don't have to say anything now
you're safe here tonight

tonight, you can
drift away

everything you're waiting for
everything you're hoping for
everything you want to keep
everything you want taken away

sleep's palace is yours tonight
in the moonlight
dream's river is yours

enfolding you in starlight
you're safe here tonight

so put it all down
tonight, you can
drift away

Like light

like the smell... of summer's mown grass
like my love's timelessness... sweetening my air
like a soft leather coat... left on memory's stair
like all of this... and much more
like the brightest light
like the lowest fire, still burning inside me...

like the moment... when these perfect memories
die
like the moment... when every perfect light
dies
comes solitude... comes grace

Another song

The snow the sun
the woodsmoke
in your voice
only make sense
outside of walls
because inside
we both knew
you couldn't see
past the death
buried in you

me, I have no use
for death
so I clear my calendar
set time aside
so I can make room
for another record
for another song

The eyes of others

I didn't betray you
the mountain is still there
the ice the stone the green
like a piano counting
every numbered breath
winter makes the light
painful too bright
for carrying those memories
of logging roads and fir
and the sweet alpine silence
I didn't betray you
I just turned away
and let the eyes of others
erase us

Shining thing

To reach the end
and begin again
in dark water
in the light
seeing every breath
and every making
the heart, the hands
waking

Black star

Come for me
flow to me, become me
grow through me
use me up

I'm not the sparrow
I want the freedom
of dust

come for me
use your name for me
call your wind, scatter me
lift me up

The fixation

A life in gray dawn
in an unpacked suitcase
in a station waiting for trains
between counting and tears
unreleased by the hard poet's light
and the trailing shadows
of imagining a forgiveness
searching the fading faces
of aging photographs
in all your obsessions
in your cage
forever asking directions
from a bed of dry river stones
and the dead

The silver forest

All the wounded
   the wandering
the returning years
   sing to us through
the stone gate
   shadows and light
my heart shines
   with song, wind plays
memory's poem
   like a silver forest
and we walk on
   together

Blue

Memory is blue, cancer
is blue, my crossing is blue
living like this is blue, longing
is blue and the leaving is blue
empty like blue, cruel like new
rain turning blue in your cooling
waiting for you is blue, seeing
as I do, me in your eyes so blue
because memory is blue
and remembering you breaks
my careful prison of true, blue
I imagine my hands have made
you, because in my dreaming I touch
your blue, breathing I taste you
my angel, your wings so blue
singing, you waiting for blue
dying I wait for you, but nothing
is more than blue, more than you

Rice

When you look at rice
do you believe in god?

Midstream

Like a horse
    standing cold midstream
that feeling of time
    like a broken window
you can smell it
    soft dust in the air
souls in the fall light
    the changing water
holding the breath fast
    that horse he was yours
but I'm the only one
    who remembers

From my notebook II

To get to freedom: softly, *softly*... push out your boat, point it away from the shore, pull your coat closer around your collar, *let go*... and set your course to someplace *beyond* fear.

Coming for you

Don't fall into the fire
don't ask why
don't walk away
don't count the days
don't look down
that sound you're hearing
through the mirrors of ordinary rain, now
that's the sound of something new
not yesterday and not tomorrow, now
it will return, a bright day
and all that perfect summer green
and the bright unbroken blue
coming through
back from memory's house
from the eyes of infinity
coming for you

Faded light

Love is naming me tonight
pain and all that remains
in my memory
like rain scattered birds
like sun blistered paint
so I give more away
because that's what you do
at high tide breaking through
salt wind cutting exhausted wire
everywhere the smell of faded light
scattered on my floor
so I use my hands
to hold bitter surrender
I use my heart
when I don't want to remember

Let it be gone

Let it be gone
all the night's tearful rain
blown through open windows
the snow the ice
the shadows of stone
the pull of the bow the strings all sound
reflections and empty glass and footsteps
the heartbeat of every road
the naming of mountains
with my heavy breath exhaling
let it be gone
let it be carried away by crows
or on the wind the tide or gravity
let it drift away from our memory
let's forget its real name
hidden in a burning forest
smoke and fear and wounds
let it slip from my hands
into drying summer grass
let it be gone

Out in the stars

Felt the stars
fill my arm
felt their impatient
arrangements pulling
me out the open window
into their open heart

silently walking me back
into the sparrow's
darkness with no
weight of returning
no light no hearing
no dreams no *here*

but then came my sad
crashlanding back
right back here again
everything as broken
on the floor like before

felt the stars
leaving me below
for this terrible thing
I don't want now
leaving all my hours
crawling on the floor
and every window
closed

Untitled fragments

I dream about a small boat
painted blue

in my dream the boat is coming for me
the boat is you

I dream I put my name on a stone
put the stone in a field

in my dream you say forget all the names
make the stone your home

I dream everyone is wearing black
but not you

Still, on warm summer nights
the familiar smell of the warming grass

returns to remind me of my time with you
reminds me of our walks beside the lake

and still, I dream about our small boat
painted blue floating in our quiet sea

I still dream that you're coming for me
in my dream the boat is us

You never ask, I never speak

I hear a drum beating in my mind
there's something I left undone

I never asked, I never spoke, I hear words beating
in my blood, there's something I wanted undone

we never see, we never know, I hear a killer beating
in my heart, there's something I lost tonight

we never win, do we? we never dream really, I hear
  an angel
speaking about how lonely it is to be an angel
there's something new being born tonight

stay go
go stay
I don't care anymore. I still want you to know
  everything
I still want you to see me, I still love something
  about you
I still hate you, I don't care anymore

There was an old man who lived beside a cold, clear
mountain lake. Every morning he woke, alone, cold.
He built a fire, his fingers moving slowly. He made tea.
Then, he put on his old coat and walked beside the quiet
lake. The sun rose over the mountains and turned the
motionless lake water into a mirror. The old man stopped
to look across the glassy water. His eyes became mirrors.
The beauty stopped his heart, for just a second. In that
second, he was dead. Then, he walked back to the fire.

And he wrote it all down, how it felt to be completely empty.

Someone was in my heart
someone left my heart
I no longer know these words I see
inside my thoughts
is there really hope?
is there really a future?
is dreaming real?

What is my name?

Thoughts at night

I say the same things
over and over to myself
I wish I could talk to you tonight
for hours and hours and hours

*

about poems and prisons
about prayers and fears
about how hard we drive ourselves
and about how after midnight
doubt is all we allow ourselves

*

I wish I could talk to you tonight
for hours and hours and hours
I think I understand now
what we keep and what we leave out
about lies and emptiness
about loves and silences

*

but I just say the same things
over and over to myself
I wish I could talk to you tonight
for hours and hours and hours
I just wish we could talk

Checking for angels

Just
checking for angels
trembling inside and tired
I don't think
we need to explain
where we're going
or where we've been

*

life
is a poem about dying
learning to be part of something
rising while we're still living

just
checking for angels
trembling inside and tired

I don't think
I can pretend I hear birds singing
when I hear voices in the dawn

*

love
is a poem about trying
a yearning to glow
burning and undefeated

just
checking for angels
trembling inside and tired

I don't think
I can bear to add
any more longing to my voice

*

joy
is a poem about saying no
when yes means dying
for the memory of who you were

I'm just
checking for angels
trembling inside and tired

so
write me your warnings and
write me your sad songs and
tell me all about
the love you never had
tonight, I'm just
checking for angels
trembling inside and tired

All for your name

There is a small annoying
war someplace in my breathing
the endless talking and talking
like it means something, talking
an exhausted obvious chorus
of repetition meant for hiding
but duller, more boring, avoiding
something, turning every sound
into a stirring, into a storm
outside the neighbor's air
conditioner sucks the icy winter air
into its metal lung to freeze
darker rooms that cannot possibly
be too warm under this frozen starless night
I listen to both of our metal voices
for the moment in my heart
which hasn't come yet
and probably never will
when I can just stop everything
even this scribbling, and say your name
out loud, the electrifying truth
of what it means to say your burning name
out loud, for me, for the weary chorus
for some honesty in my exhausted life
to speak, be heard to speak, to lift
this terrible cold terrifying weight
to finally be free as the dust

Places in my heart

I have no house
not the way you think
of houses or questions
about houses
the answers I miss most are
doors painted shut years ago
those houses
were burned down anyway
out of meanness I think
you told me once
how to escape from all of this
from remembering funerals
photographs in wallets
perfect houses
stories and repeating myself
but that was years ago
and I forgot what you said

Prayer wheel

Turning
inside out
everyone I know
is losing it tonight, fucking losing it
tonight, the cold coming down, unbidden
on me, us our terrible unbearable
the new normal, silent, empty century
doors locking behind me
the smallest things pressing me down
while your memory glows, just out there
my stone-cold sadness, me abandoning
turn me fucking inside out

so I pray, please turn back
fix this, whatever the fuck it is, broken
heart please, turn just turn just
come back
please come back
because all of it, is wrong
because all of it, I can't face it
the ending the forgetting, softly
even the smallest touch
not even the smallest victory
like the sound of your voice
I never recorded

so turn around, please
turn around
just turn around
so I can feel
so I can see

here, one more time
one more time
just
one more time
you you you

Untitled fragment II

Because tonight our love
true love
is the color of blood
and belongs to the sea

because tonight our memory
begins its dreaming
returning everything, *everything*
forever grateful

The fall

If you think about
everything you drop
breaking hard
on the cold dark ground
using up all of your love
in the falling down
breaking what you love
breaking what you thought you found

if you think about
everything you start
making a living hard
on the cold dark ground
using up all of your trust
in your half-lived life
alone, to be ground down
lost, to burn your last hope down

you want it to stop
you want it to let you sleep
just one night through
you want it to let you be
you long for it to stop

but, you can't return
and you can't decide
and you can't stop the falling

you just want to feel it less inside
you just want to hide
see each day through
when you can, you pray to live
and when you can't, you pray to die

*

so you go on thinking
about everything you drop
breaking hard
on the cold dark ground
using up all of your love
in every memory, falling
breaking what you love
breaking what you thought you found

until you can't remember
why you loved, or why

you still can't remember
what it feels like
to be light
and what it must feel like
to be someone else

Winter

Written in your color
of the low winter light
deep in the river
another perfect moment passing
away
into a black door

*

Written in your color
of the low winter night
deep in your heavy sleep now
another perfect dream passing
away
into a black door

*

Tell me about your love
tell me all about the color of your love
then hold your breath
then hold me in the soft rhythm
of your breath
we'll be going through the black door
and it will keep, it will keep

*

Written in your color
of the low winter light
deep in the river
another perfect moment passing
away
into the black door

Lost and found

Our love should be a keeper's thing
so far away from the damaged road
that took so long to get us here, stumbling

like we all do, because it's who we really are
worried runners and not the brave fighters
we tell ourselves we could be, we know distance

but can't work out what it means to stand perfectly
still and tell the truth about what we put in our blood
night after night, to just get us out of here, like tonight

out of all the shit we get ourselves into, but
tonight, just sit next to me and put your head
on my shoulder and put your hand

in my hand and put your broken heart
in my unsure heart while the frost and the stars do
their best to melt into something warm, like a promise

we can both keep, for us, for ourselves, to feel trust
again, deeply, to stay and never
leave

*

I know all my broken places by name
I just can't face who I'm becoming in my darkening
memory, revealed but still concealed
by who I accidentally
became

Memories on a map

You are dead
and I am dead
under a soft falling snow
outside covering, what the storm left, behind
and places we'll never see, ahead
you are dead
and so am I...

the stars in winter night
feel colder than
our heavy blanket
of silence and places we'll never see
now we're just memories on a map
the stars in winter night
feel colder in the dark...

you were afraid
I was afraid
and the indifferent sea
that brought us all here
waits patiently for everyone
you were afraid
and so was I...

now you are home
and I am home
tired of the living and us, gone
no longer their concern
time takes everyone, all the same
finally, you are home
and so am I...

Safe

This cool glass night
this wind, this uncertain light
speak to me low
like fire
my memory is a monk
safe in a house of roses
my eyes are a song
about roads, dust
about a burning river
unbidden, yet returning
forever

The beauty of rain

All night my memory
just words torn
from your eyes
strike my windows
exhausted by my
longing

you return, every night
silent now, waiting for me
to predict whether
I should guess or not
alone with my thoughts
like broken stars

me, dying in my years
and the beauty of rain
I'm ready

Return to blue

Down to the blessed
end there's a garden
and a soft rain failing
on me
and there's the blessed
pardon waiting
for all my stupid
dead ends forgiven given
like this soft rain falling
on me

down to the blessed
end there's you
and the promise
of the burning
of dust
of golden stars inside us
and the blessed eventual return
to blue

Cold wave

Black angel, scars
for wings, stars for eyes,
my blind hate for blood
cut me down, put my love
in the ground, put a stone
where my heart should be
you, my cold wave, come
be my song, cut me down

Tonight

Somehow, the snow
remembers, I forget how
it doesn't matter, *now*
is braver than tomorrow

One time tender

Walking out into night
I remember you like a jar
of rain, paint peeling
from our empty house
clouds tonight same as day
you'd say, I'm left behind
you won't come back
to burn my letters
to give away my clothes
my eyes are filled with you
my home, one time tender

Playlist
"One for My Baby (And One More for the Road)" (Frank Sinatra), "All I Want" (Lore City), "Someone to Watch Over Me" (Etta James), "Someones" (Adna), "Someone Will Pay" (Justin Townes Earle), "Edit the Sad Parts" (Modest Mouse), "Does Someone Have Your Baby Now" (Mazzy Star), "I Want Someone Badly" (Jeff Buckley), "Cold Desert" (Kings of Leon)

Standing in the dark

Standing in the dark
listening to "Jesus Alone"
the doors of my heart
started opening again
the candle that was once
mine, went out, yes, but
what I owe for this opening
I will owe, but for you, you —
choose a door, and come

How words fit together

Cancer changes how words fit together in the mind. It's a problem for a writer. Ideas become severe, even brutal, to match my mood. Sometimes the things I say surprise me. Sometimes it takes days to remember what I said to someone, and then feel stupid, or feel regret for saying what I said. And those thoughts make me feel less human somehow, or *more* human. Unfiltered. I can't decide which. I get frozen in that place of not knowing.

It's an earthy journey, cancer treatment. Basic, something drawn into you by the soil. A returning impulse to something *elemental*. To be broken down into constituent parts. I think about grass, and molecules. I notice how the fall light adds a golden tint to everything, even sidewalks and green things. Ugly things become beautiful.

I have to decide day to day just how much fight I have in me. For anything. Some days I surprise myself by finding I have very little fight left. And I don't care.

The memory

Every age presents the promise
that we can begin again
gently, softly, as the late snow melts
as birdsong fills the quiet mind
something innocent in the air
like the idea of a welcoming god
like the sound of a broom on stone
we step lightly so as to not disturb
the memory

Sweet talk

I stopped in the rain and died, I spoke
my last words to the rain, to the rain,
when I said goodbye to the sparrows
goodbye, our time is like silver, like silver
I heard someone sing once, not gold
go on my love, go on

Angel

I dreamt last night
of you writing all these amazing songs
and a shadow standing over my bed
a dark angel, like you
softly speaking a warning
and I woke with a start
like I should know the angel
thinking I could never remember
all those amazing songs
but somehow you can, you do
how do you do it?
and the moonlight filled my head
and I could hear the Ohio River
and your eyes burned in my memory
like two cigarettes
burning white in the dark
it was that real

Turning home

Tonight, your story
begins its quiet unfolding
holding everything, everything
together

tonight, your worry
begins its soft receding
leaving everything, everything
forever grateful, but still too far away

because tonight your love
true love
is the color of blood
and belongs to the sea

because tonight your memory
begins its dreaming
returning everything, everything
forever grateful, but still too far away

just wait
one day, one day soon
you will wake, turn home
and you will feel, you will feel it
you will be happy
once again

From darkness to darkness

Awake, the river of stars awaken
unknowable, like the silence of birds flown
paused, like a prayer unspoken, for one flight
of perfect sleep

all my thoughts hide in darkness
leaving any escaping light a broken thing

I wrote you a long letter
but I didn't post it, instead I burned it
all of it, sparks almost the shapes of my words
unreadable fireflies

still, I want to remember this day
like a time before the breaking
like a finger on a scar
like smoke from a cooling fire

Late walk in winter

I.

At the end of love there's love
I hope it's true

II.

I care when I'm bleeding
otherwise I don't

III.

What we have is what we have
a late walk in winter

Purity

Throughout
    this movement
ethereal, physical
    suffering, joy
a sound like bronze
    hands like grace
moving me into song
    I can't cry
but I want to

Death in the age of texting

Out there
just out there
you and your number
a very small space
closed now, exhausted
a faint rose smell on the air
a memory's passing breath
I can't remember your face

Empty

Testing my belief
when I'm afraid I pray to live
I ask the soft stars for strength for sight
I want to be free to feel memory again
I ache to live in an etched golden light

failing faith my hope my love
when I'm strong I pray to die
I ask the cold for ice for an end to dreams
I want to be gone to fall forever into darkness
I ache for an empty starless night

Untitled fragment III

When I got cancer, it was like
I sailed far out to sea in a small
boat. Back then, it was a feeling of
safety, escape, my practice now, is
somehow to let my boat dissolve
to accept that that is what it's like
to be alive in this world, present
in this world, human

but every day, I ask myself
am I'm really that brave?

All the bad words

All the bad words
storm the shore
night after night
cutting the air
into dawn
there's no arguing
no more longing
just the carrying
the counting
just the living
as they die in the rain
the bad words
every sharp meaning
cold in the heart
now a part
of us, souvenir
done close
they stick to us
warm like memory
of every day's
dying hours
dark houses
and scars

Almost falling

I remember you almost falling
into emptiness and thinking
the air should have wings
like the blood has memories
like when the music bites
hard it almost feels like
bells ringing in darkness
announcing your burial
over and over like
your final hour of the light
but the true nature of falling
is more like a frightened
bird's flight through an open window
than the weight of your name
carved in stone

Lines soften

All our lines soften into a memory
of who we were, an imitation
slowly dissolving into who we will be
when all the doors open into night

Playlist
"Unchained Melody (A Cappella Version)" (The Fleetwoods), "Ain't No Love in the Heart of the City" (Bobby "Blue" Band), "Cosmic Dancer" (Nick Cave), "Goin' Home" (Malcolm Holcombe), "Lungs" (Steve Earle), "My Hometown" (North Mississippi Allstars), "You on the Run" (The Black Angels), "Baby Please Don't Go" (Billy Gibbons and The BFG's), "Feel Alright" (Steve Earle), "One Big Love" (Emmylou Harris), "Something Within" (Buddy Miller/Julie Miller/The McCrary Sisters), "Racing in the City" (Justin Townes Earle), "Dear God, Please Help Me" (Marianne Faithfull), "You Got to Move" (North Mississippi Allstars), "Back in My Day" (The Handsome Family), "Something on Your Mind" (Kyle Craft), "Mambo Sun" (Sean Ono Lennon & Charlotte Kemp Muhl), "Fly, My Sweet Dove" (Will Johnson)

A fire in dry grass

Like a virgin
I tremble, I count
the dying minutes before
I merge with you, knowing
our fire will consume us both
our skin will burn new
and your night, like every memory
will last, will be yours, forever
and my prayer, like dry grass
to burn, to return, to rise
will be mine

Soft as skin

You are exquisite
in your dream
of blue jazz
with soft green eyes
the waves touching
you beyond glass
cupping the sun
just below your chin
making the smallest
memory smile golden
walking half waking
at your scented
edges, soft as skin

The pool

Inside you, the sea returns
to me, soft as your eyes
the memory of your perfect light
held like breath, the pool
where we lose our lives
and combine, turning over
to live again, to die, to let go
of words, of time, of memory

Playlist
"Come Over" (Lydia Loveless), "Red Dirt Girl" (Emmylou Harris), "I Came Here to Feed You" (Erica Freas), "Sign of the Judgement" (Cassandra Wilson), "Go Ahead On" (Robert Belfour), "40 Days in Kansas" (Ezra Furman), "Drawn Away" (Fruit Bats), "Rooks (Live)" (Shearwater), "This Is Desire" (Hugo Race Fatalists), "Tangled Up in Love" (The Rifles), "Tell Me Why" (Alejandro Escovedo), "Wash Off" (Foals), "Juanita" (Sheryl Crow/Emmylou Harris), "Broken Promise Ring" (The Ataris), "Down Past the Bottom" (Lucinda Williams), "Back to You" (Psychic Ills), "She Could Never Resist a Winding Road" (Richard Thompson), "Goodnight Goodnight" (Spiritualized)

A place to start

The door hasn't opened for an age
but it will, and in that hour, though late
will still be ours, that day, though far
away, will be like spring, and the wood
doves will return, with the smell of forest
a new green, from a starry place of waiting
will open, and everything we can name
will wake, will stay, will be, will speak
and we'll walk through the door, on that day

Ohio

I can still hear you, saying
dark water is always pulling
us like the road, blood deep
into our dreams and scars
a train passed over the Ohio
and moaned, I remember
you said the sound of trains
made you feel so alone
your eyes heavy in the saying
like river soil, wet, deep
filled with stars
that night you spoke of her
a woman called *Memory*
it's been years, but
even now, I remember you said
every time she returned
her soft green eyes toward you
you had to look away, but
that was then, not today
not today

Playlist
"La Jeune Fille en Feu" (Para One & Arthur Simonini), "Witches' Song" (Marianne Faithfull), "Shadows & Doubts" (Lucinda Williams), "The Dark End of the Street" (James Carr), "No Treasure but Hope" (Tindersticks), "Just Wait" (Blues Traveler), "Xanax Baby" (Jessica Says), "Done Bleeding" (The Mountain Goats), "Bird Without a Feather" (North Mississippi Allstars), "Soul on Fire" (Spiritualized),

"Crippled & Crazy" (Scott H. Biram), "Satellite of Love" (Joseph Arthur), "I Asked for Water (He Gave Me Gasoline)" (Lucinda Williams), "She" (Over the Rhine), "Mercenary World" (Holy Sons), "I Want You to Be My Love" (Over the Rhine), "Love Is Blindness" (Cassandra Wilson), "Farewell" (Rosie Thomas)

Singing still

I want to softly run my fingers
over your painted rose
remembering all of your songs
unheard but written on the clouds
that breathless ache in your light
slipping under a copper sky
hand to hour, hand to heart
I remember it all, every taste
and your golden rose, with one
perfect tear of blood-red
memory, chipped, but singing still

Playlist
"Goodbye" (Emmylou Harris), "Falls" (The Cave Singers), "I'm Your Man" (Nick Cave), "Hunter's Moon" (Thin White Rope), "She's Got You (Single Version)" (Loretta Lynn), "Suck the Blood from My Wound" (Ezra Furman), "Bossy" (JD McPherson), "Changes Come" (Over the Rhine), "Heroin" (Joseph Arthur), "Paradise" (Alejandro Escovedo), "Sweet Talk" (Spiritualized), "Heart Disease" (The Helio Sequence), "Fast and Loose" (The Rich Hands), "If It Be Your Will" (Antony), "At the Cut" (The Cave Singers), "Hold On" (Alabama Shakes), "Final Prayer" (The Men), "Sad Days Lonely Nights" (Spritualized), "Cigarettes in the Rain" (Vandoliers), "Soul on Fire" (Spiritualized), "Lately" (The Helio Sequence), "Almost Blue" (Chet Baker)

Beside the blue lake

You were a warm summer afternoon
a soft summer dress, so light
that being alive was a timeless thing
like the fragrance of an orange,
a bowl of honey, a song of new green
from heart to memory now, alive
beside a blue lake, in a forest of stars

Like fire

Entering into you, the rhythm
of your night-heart beats out my
belief in god for love, I taste your blood
I breathe your release, our words burn
away, and we're bound together
forever, to dissolve then to rise, like fire
to burn pain away, curling in the cooling
coal-bright air, to shiver time into dust
to shiver us into dust

Playlist
"Like a Bird" (Mondo Cozmo), "King of Dust" (The Handsome Family), "Can't Hardly Wait" (The Ataris), "Helpless" (Buffy Saint-Marie), "Pray the Devil Back to Hell" (Lucinda Williams), "Too Late" (Guantanamo Baywatch), "She's Got You" (Kyle Craft), "Love Blues" (Hugo Race and Michelangelo Russo), "Be Quiet and Drive (Far Away) (Acoustic Version)" (Deftones), "Guilt (Mix)" (Marianne Faithfull), "More Dead" (Death Valley Girls), "Sweet Talk" (Spiritualized), "Cigarette (Age of Innocence)" (Mondo Cozmo), "12.15.10" (The Ataris), "Black Cadillac" (Mondo Cozmo), "Goodbye" (Emmylou Harris), "Burn My Shadow" (UNCLE/Ian Astbury), "Generator" (Mondo Cozmo), "American Soil" (Ezra Furman)

"Shooting Jesus"

You walked out when you were 17
but you started *shooting Jesus* at 12, all
that light lit you up, all your stars like furious
song lines, a burning that gave you a place and
a home and a family, you never thought about
growing old, that was for other people, you'd
make songs for the road, and the road would
keep you alive until every mile turned into
the same emptiness as home, and whatever room
was as good as any to be your last, just you and
Jesus, your needle, and your final song, your last
breath slipping from silence to silence and beyond

Wanderer

I am a pilgrim in your eyes
a useless wanderer, praying for more time
and for more road, but prayer today
is like melting ice

some songs we sing into bone
scrimshaw, carved with lost maps and lives
we sing on because we're all empty
longing to be filled

I hold you in my memory as I walk
a perfect white rose in moonlight, your
wet petals dropping one by one
into my mouth

Playlist
"Glory Days" (Justin Townes Earle), "Long Time Comin'" (Bruce Springsteen), "Downbound Train" (Joe Pug), "Dollar Bill Blues" (Townes Van Zandt), "John the Revelator" (Scott H. Biram), "No Surrender" (Holly Williams), "61 Highway" (North Mississippi Allstars), "Sleeping on the Blacktop" (Colter Wall), "Hit the River" (Scott H. Biram), "I'll Trade You Money for Wine" (Robbie Fulks), "God Fearing People" (Legendary Shack Shakers), "When the Way Gets Dark" (Lucinda Williams), "Outlaw State of Mind" (Chris Stapleton), "Casino" (Scott H. Biram), "Bridge City Rose" (Kyle Craft), "Graceland" (Justin Townes Earle), "Rogers Park" (Justin Townes Earle), "Everything's Changed" (Patty Griffin), "I Had a Dream" (Dex Romweber), "Goodbye" (Steve Earle)

What we tell ourselves

There's a way out of all this —
(it doesn't exist)

Sand angel

She said, "hurt is a window, I see my world through it,
it's my life now." I think... she means the light makes
every place heartache, her place of sun-washed sand,
not for living in, not for love, but I hope I'm wrong,
maybe it's just her way to speak about the prison of
memory mostly late at night, like all my songs picked
and threadbare like rags, once I believed all
my lines were lions (she said they fell from the stars)
she knew the night better than me, when words
come even now, shining cool like water, but it's
a trick of the heat rising in the hot distance of
time, sand angels I call them, when I speak
her name just before sleep, I say the same things
to her I was never brave enough to say out loud
now that she's gone, I can't explain, but it's always
her there as I drift off to sleep, she became one
of my sand angels, silent, watching, she's there
every time I write, too, I wonder... will she forgive me
once I find the words to tell her story, our story,
and all I failed to do

The promise

Driving away from you
through a darkening tunnel of towering trees
islands and goodbyes flying high above me
every song of yours ringing in every nerve

broken hearted in this sailing wind
that sings no rain but reveals how it still carries
silver words strong as ice and the promise
of fire of smoke imitating wings

driving back toward you
I know my road will burn me free
of doubt of my self-obsessive counting
of every heavy breath that will one day

be my road to rest

Glass

Time is glass, soft like air
with the promise of sky, of you
of water without words
or sometimes all the breaking
it takes to be free, to be a city
alone, to be new, to see forever
or to just let go because
time is like glass, and love
is a prayer, touching every stone
every branch, every river
braided together into one

Ashes

The parting of your sound
the dying of your candle
walking alone into my memory
cold stars and a facing moon
love has left me in amber
out of tide, wounded, new
numbed by all this counting
of what was once forever, done
now, these ashes in my mind
turned over, not home, not you

Into the hardest night

You can hear it on the walls
scratching to get in, scratching
my name on the rocks, on the wind
on my skin, the stories I can
prove, and the stories I can't —
I'm going deeper and deeper
into the circle, deeper and deeper
into the hardest night, I'm blind
but I'm singing — and all my burning —
for you, *my soul*, for you, because lies
burn with the same heat as truth

Playlist
"If I Live or If I Die" (Cuff the Duke), "Ain't Blues Too Sad" (Roky Erickson), "Don't Stand at the Stove" (Bobby Bare, Jr.), "Never Comin' Home" (Scott H. Biram), "Verlaine Shot Rimbaud" (Lydia Loveless), "Cannery Row" (Deadstring Brothers), "Roll On" (Dex Romweber Duo), "What's Done Is Done" (Jack White), "Gonna Miss You When You're Gone" (Patty Griffin), "Everything Is Broken" (R.L. Burnside), "Heartbreak Junky" (Kyle Craft), "Don't Cry Baby" (Etta James), "Turn It Up/Arbaden" (Robert Plant), "Day I Die" (The National), "Divers of the Dust" (Marissa Nadler), "Whitest Boy on the Beach" (Fat White Family), "Meet Me in the Alleyway" (Steve Earle), "Sandy" (Dream Police)

Sleep will come

Your moonlight heart
    a folded life, so near crying
like a cooling star, an empty glass
    set beside a wedding ring
a broken pocketknife, a forgotten key
    a box full of boxes
paper angels and loose change
    hush, sleep will come
to your frightened hands, your hidden eyes
    all your dreams dreamed
rest now, let it be, go

These memories

Standing by your river, names flow by
some I remember, some are fading
now, into the turning dark water, can you

hear me, or are you speeding away, too
downstream, as I rise to these memories
but I can't hold, I need to see the shapes

again, before the memory comes, I can't
see, I can't feel the future, and this cold
river is leaving without me, endlessly

Night

Night, I achieve oblivion, shadows
inside a forest, border my memories,
voiceless, receding, a home for my
home, honesty in breathing, rhythmic
emptiness, night, dissolving lines
from blame

this way is old, it was built stone
by stone, by hands other than mine
here now, I can't remember my name
and I don't care, this darkness
comes easily, through open doors
bringing regrets, knives, smoke
and songs

Broken stones

Somewhere a house is falling down
into a song about empty rooms and
stories about time running out and
dear god, it's exhausting saying all
these words again, but words break
open all the miles I've slept through

so I repeat them, heavy as they are
the house you build won't be the house
you'll live in, no, just more stories piled
on stories, some you'll write down
some you'll repeat to yourself, until
you move again, using rivers as maps

always there's a house in your sleep
but that's not where this story ends
no, this will end in a place where every
color will be black, even the butterflies
and you'll wish you planned it all better
but this is what you'll get, almost free

at the end, but this place will be filled with
dark shapes you can't name, like wind flowing
over dry fields, words carved on broken
stones you can only read by touching them

Playlist
"To Love Somebody" (Janis Joplin), "Are You Alright?"
(Lucinda Williams), "We Struggle" (Malcolm Holcombe),
"Hippy Gumbo" (Beth Orton), "Attack of the Killer Bees"

and "Rental Sting" (Archers of Loaf), "Christchurch Woman" (Justin Townes Earle), "How Many Worlds" (Marianne Faithfull/Teddy Thompson), "Is This How We End Up?" (The Ataris), "All Souls' Day" (The Ataris), "Shivers" (Divine Fits), "Skeleton Key" (Mark Lanegan), "Clear Blue Eyes" (Amos Lee/Lucinda Williams), "Untitled 2" (The Shivers), "I Shall Be Released" (Jack Johnson with ALO), "Favorite Time of Light (Acoustic Version from Nowhere Farm)" (Over the Rhine), "Lose Yourself" (Black Rebel Motorcycle Club)

To die

Pain the traveler, my angel
time for me to go, to die
in my worry, in my mind
in my echo, in my staying —

pain the borrower, my prayer
asking for more, to die
in my love, in my touch
in my silence, in my ache

my angel, time for me to go

Playlist
"Fresh New Eyes" (Brainiac), "Easy Come, Easy Go" (Marianne Faithfull), "Dreaming of" (Foals), "Summer of '42" (Kishi Bashi), "Soldier" (The Groundhogs), "The Night David Bowie Died" (Lilly Hiatt), "Soldier's Song" (Lucinda Williams), "Suitcase" (Over the Rhine), "Don't Let Me Die in Florida" (Patty Griffin), "Roadrunner" (Thin White Rope), "Rattlesnake Highway" (Palma Violets), "No I in Threesome" (Interpol), "Closer" (Thunderbitch), "Bar Italia" (Pulp), "Midnight Run" (Willie Nelson), "The Part of Him" (Drive-By Truckers), "Way It Is, Way It Could Be" (The Weather Station), "Tonight Will Be Fine" (Teddy Thompson)

The cooling heart

How quickly the feeling fades
the source of love in a time
of wandering, the angry forest
that the mind becomes, songs
of birds come in storms, like rain,
are they confused or ecstatic, I don't
know, there is a hole someplace
where all feeling is dreaming
away, fall is here, and with it falling
hours, like leaves, to rot, to rise again
maybe, it's all beyond imagining
this long night, a language of warnings,
wings, and the cooling heart for hope

Breath of the stars

I sleep now to join the past,
the fall of sleep, walking through
old churchyards where once I
slept outside on warm summer
afternoons, soft grass and bird-
song, now waking is the hard part
dreams are years lived, and
down below the surface of time
the dead wait impatiently for
night, the breath of the stars, the
only light in the stone of eternity

Playlist
"Take It with Me" (Angie McMahon), "Christmas Card from a Hooker in Minneapolis" (The Ataris), "Pray the Devil Back to Hell" (Lucinda Williams), "Sacrificial" (Wooden Wand), "The Revenant" (Hiss Golden Messenger), "I'm Your Man" (Spiritualized), "Every Grain of Sand" (Emmylou Harris), "On Your Way" (Alabama Shakes), "A Gentle Awakening" and "You Must Have Met Little Caroline?" (JD McPherson), "Reno" (Bruce Springsteen), "After I Made Love to You" (Bonnie "Prince" Billy), "The Void" (Jay Farrar/Benjamin Gibbard), "Traveling Light" (Leonard Cohen), "Never Any Good" (Leonard Cohen), "Love in Vain" (Eric Clapton), "Distant Sky" (Nick Cave & The Bad Seeds), "Here I Am" (Emmylou Harris)

At the end of my time

Someday, my eyes will say more than my words ever could, but what they will say will be confusing to others. I will not speak anymore then. My thoughts will be dark, of machines, and chaste. At the end of each day, depleted, I will be gratefully crushed into sleep by my companion, fear, knowing that I served these final days with all of my physical strength. What I do will make others neither happy nor sad. My dreams will long for pools of perfect, clear water. But they won't find any. My dreams will become the dreams of others. As the light slowly fades, as I lie in bed each night, one perfect crystalline tear will slowly soak into my pillow. At the end of my time, however long I have left, everything I acquired in this life will be gathered up and burned, to make room for whatever comes next.

The whole world is a scene: About Goat Palace

Goat Palace is a music-documentary project by John Ellison, based in Anacortes, Washington. Our mission is to photograph and write about music and musicians, to showcase records and ideas, the objects of music, like music magazines of old once did.

We review records we love (why bother writing about music you *don't* like?), interview musicians, and cover live shows. We like to blend the arts whenever possible, which is why you'll see lots of photos, quotations, and even poetry from time to time.

The music industry is in a period of radical change, like pretty much everything else in our lives, in our communities, in our world. It's important for fans to know how hard it is for musicians to make their livings from their art. It's important to remain human, to be kind.

For musicians

First, *thank you* for doing what you do. We wouldn't be able to do what *we* do without you. The Palace is about creating an ecosystem with recording artists, building long-term relationships with the artists we love through reviews, interviews, photos, performance coverage, shared tracks, videos, and other editorial highlights. The best relationships feel *mutual*.

We'd rather have a few *deep relationships* with a few artists than a zillion superficial contacts. No one needs more noise. We *desperately* need more authentic community! That said, we do have a few things we'd like you to consider if you want us to consider writing about your latest cool release.

- We don't get paid to do this work (it's a *love thing*), so the things that add value the most — *for us* — from musicians are some sort of media (especially physical media, if you have any): CDs, cassette tapes, LPs, as well as digital downloads. Yes, we love getting downloads, too. This might sound like an odd ask in 2022, but we started out as a vinyl record label. So artifacts rule in The Palace.

- We *must* have a press release — of some kind — from *you* introducing yourself and giving us some background on what you're all about (if you're a band, include your band members' names, producer, studio, *anything* you think is cool to mention). Why your record is cool. How it was made. The *story,* as you see it.

    This also means a selection of cool band photos (include names of photographers if you want us to credit them). Speeds up the process. (*Yes,* we can dig a lot of this information out of the internet ourselves, but there are never enough hours in the day!)

- Writing about a recording artist is really about being able to introduce your work to others. This means it's important to have your music where we can link to it and share it with our readers. We prefer Bandcamp because it's an artist-friendly platform. We want our readers to consider buying your work if we write about it (if you release physical media, we want to send readers to preferably Indie record shops, like The Business in Anacortes). But Bandcamp is cool, too.

- Getting *song lyrics*, if they're not on Bandcamp, makes our job a whole lot easier. We *love* quoting lyrics from cool songs, highlighted tracks, etc. Help us out and share them with us, if you have them. You'd be surprised how easy it is for us to guess a line *wrong*.

- We're not into music streaming platforms like Spotify, Google Play, Pandora, Grooveshark, or even SoundCloud. There are a lot of reasons for this. We spin records! And cassette tapes, I mean, how cool! Besides, it's just how we are.

- Finally, interviews.

   We like to talk. If we ask for an interview, we don't submit questions to artists in advance.

   The fun of doing an interview is getting to talk to an artist we're into. Makes sense if you think about it. Artists are cool! If we do an interview, it will be live via phone (not Zoom, so you can wear whatever and be wherever). It will last about 20 to 30 minutes. We'll record our talk and use whatever fits for the post.

   If you're not into that whole thing, that's cool. We still love you.

For PR staff and labels representing musicians

Please send us a digital download of your client's music. The more tempting the submission, the more eager we'll be to jump in and support your client. Pointing us to an online streaming service is boring.

For writers interested in contributing pieces

If you want to write for The Palace, that's amazing! Our dream has been to grow this publication into an old-school music-review hub. That said, for the time being, we're a classic *no-budget* zine. We do what we do out of a deep belief that new music is exciting, and that there's an endless supply of cool new recording artists coming up.

- We don't pay anything for writing (sorry). We buy our "ruined world" anchor artwork (unless we create it ourselves), from commercial sites like Adobe Stock and Shutterstock. We also use free services like Unsplash. We credit everyone we can.

- We do have style guidelines. If you get in touch with us, and if we vibe with each other, we'll send you our style guide. Don't worry, it's not complicated, but we do have some basic (and ever-evolving) rules we try to follow.

- We don't publish snarky negative reviews. I mean, why? We don't give records star or numeric ratings. Again, why? The best negative review, in our opinion, is no review. Thousands of new records are released every day. We have our hands full just keeping up with the hundreds of artists and records we love.

- If we accept your piece, we'll give you a byline.